For Hailey and Tessa

With special thanks to Jennifer

Henry Holt and Company, LLC
Publishers since 1866
175 Fifth Avenue
New York, New York 10010
mackids.com

Library of Congress Cataloging-in-Publication Data is available

ISBN 978-0-8050-9751-1

Henry Holt books may be purchased for business or promotional use. For information on
bulk purchases, please contact Macmillan Corporate and Premium Sales Department at
(800) 221-7945 x5442 or by e-mail at specialmarkets@macmillan.com.

First Edition—2014 / Designed by Patrick Collins
Printed in China by Toppan Leefung Printing Ltd., Dongguan City, Guangdong Province
1 3 5 7 9 10 8 6 4 2

Daytime
Nighttime

WILLIAM LOW

Henry Holt and Company
New York

What do you see
in the daytime?

Butterflies

Robins

Bumblebees

Grasshoppers

Red-tailed hawks

Beavers

Rabbits

Puppies...

...and the sun!

What do you see
at nighttime?

Fireflies

Bats

Owls

Frogs

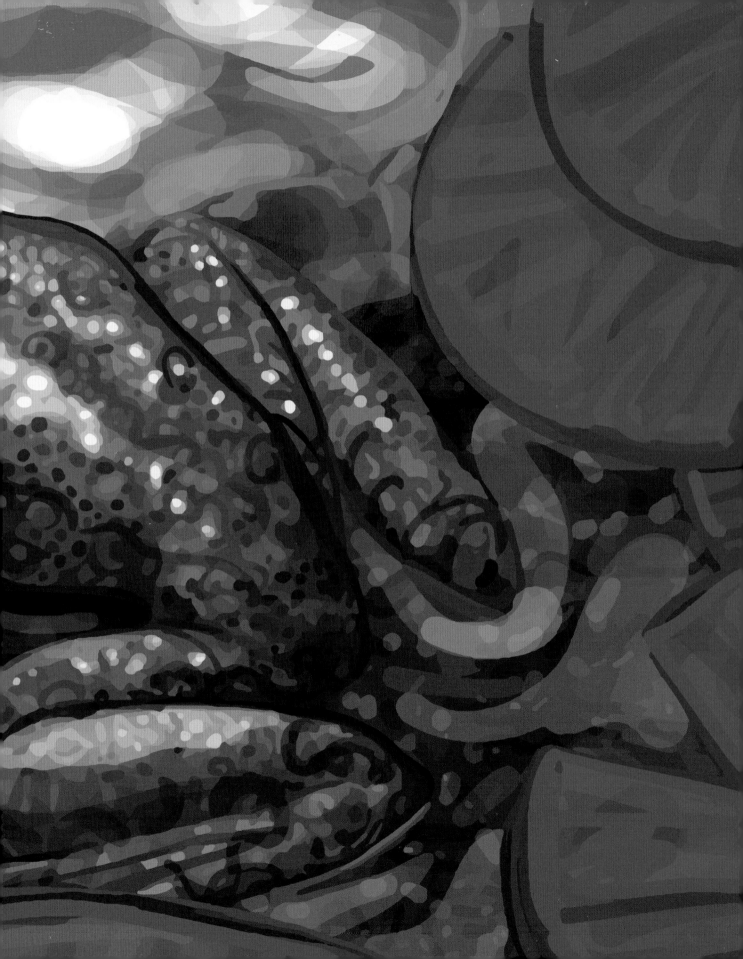

Raccoons

Teddy bears...

...and the moon!